God's Love

Alice Boschulte Murray and Diane Murray Ward

Book 1

God's Love -Book 1
Copyright © 2023 by Diane Ward
All rights reserved.
Published by Red Penguin Books
Bellerose Village, NY
ISBN 978-1-63777-425-0

No part of this book may be reproduced in any form or by any electronic or mechanical means, including information storage and retrieval systems, without written permission from the author, except for the use of brief quotations in a book review.

"God's Love" is dedicated to our wonderful family who are blessings to us both.

Holy Family

WELCOME

Introduction and Purpose

Welcome to "God's Love."

"God's Love" has been a labor of love between a mother and daughter. Both women are certified CCD curriculum instructors within elementary schools. It's a biblical journey that we hope will be both educational and inspiring.

"God's Love" consists of three children's books and a teacher's manual.

Childrens' Book
- Each one of these three children's books reference bible stories accompanied with replicable illustrations, vocabulary words and listening words.
- Vocabulary words are intended as spelling words for early education grade-levels participants.
- Listening words appear within the story and are longer than spelling words.
- Each story is intentionally succinct.
- Children books are sized for easy transport, child-friendly size and font-type.
- Drawings are intended to promote a child's retainage and referencing of stories. Drawings are provided in black and white allowing for coloring.

Teacher's Manual
- Lists Vocabulary and Listening Words.
- Proposes activities enhancing bible story themes.
- Quotes bible source for referencing.
- Exceeds story lines (in some instances).
- Reproducible black and white drawings were designed to be quick and easy, and blackboard simple. They appear only within children's books.
- We included children and women stories sometimes less familiar for inclusion.
- Reference to geography, culture and lifestyle (e.g., chores, food) are included to inspire further study and interest.
- Additional resources are encouraged

VOLUME I

God Instructs and Assures Us
Fruit of the Spirit, The Lord's Prayer, Greatest Commandment

Women and the Bible
Blessed Mary Answered Yes, Hannah, Shiprah and Puah, BVM and St. Elizabeth, Queen Esther

Nature
Garden of Eden, Calming the Wind

Relatives
My Father's House, St. Joachim and St. Anne

Bonus Closing Page: Moses and the Reeds on the River

LOVE

Trust
Peace
Kindness
Forgiveness
Friendship
Hope

God Instructs and Assures Us

"Fruit of the Spirit"

We must try everyday to love, bring joy and peace to each other.
Be patient, not mean. Be kind and be generous and share our blessings with others.

Vocabulary Words: love, joy

Listening Words: spirit, peace, fruit

Our Father...

God Instructs and Assures Us

"The Lord's Prayer"

We want to learn how to pray daily to reach God's kingdom.
We want to be forgiven our sins and eat with Jesus.

Vocabulary Words: pray, God

Listening Words: alone, daily, closer

GOD GIVEN RULES

The Ten Commandments

God Instructs and Assures Us

"The Greatest Commandment"

Love God with all your heart, and your neighbor as yourself,
with all your being and strength.
Do this and you will live.

Vocabulary Words: heart, mind, all, you

Listening Words: neighbor, yourself

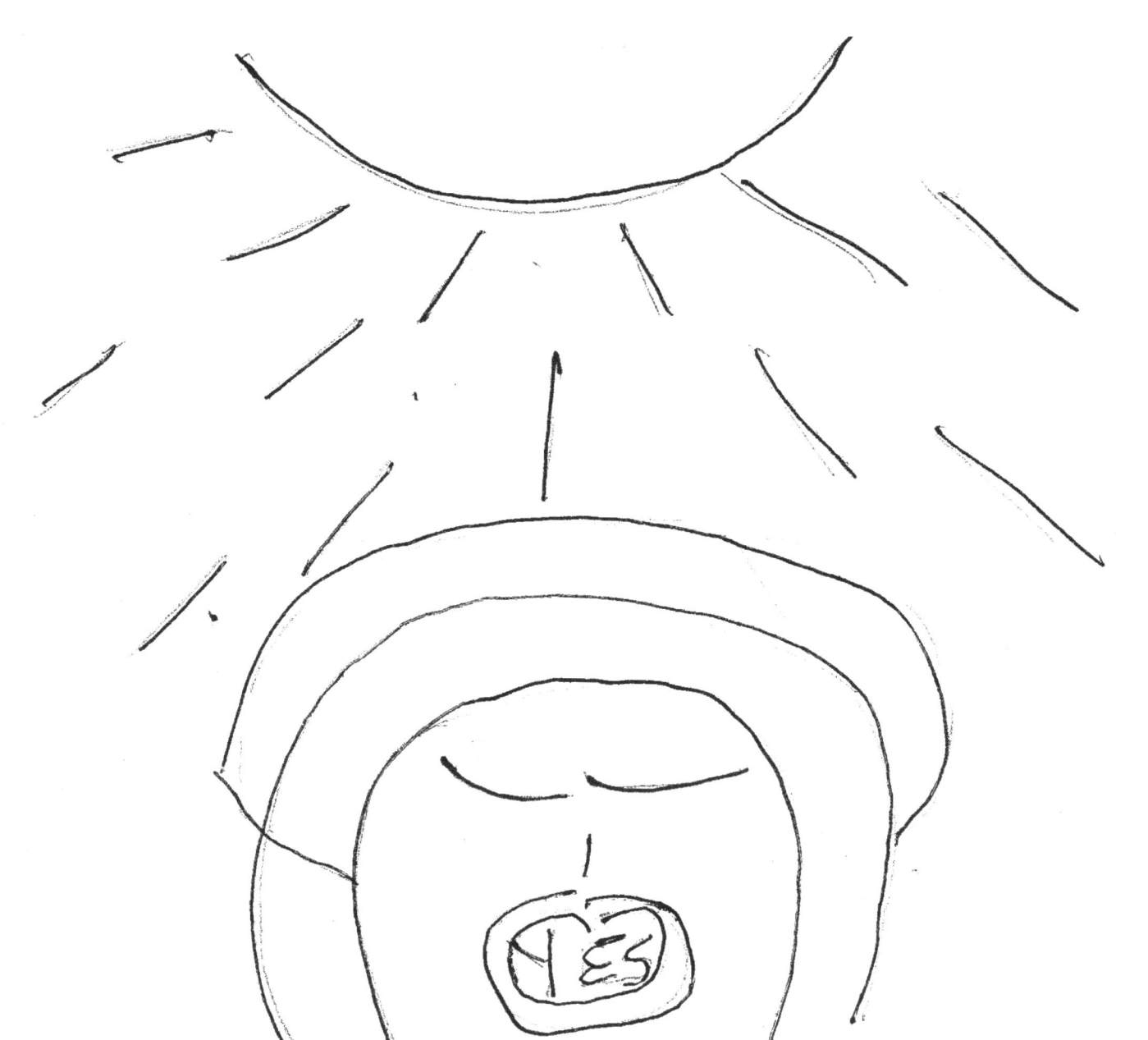

Women in the Bible

"Blessed Mary Answered Yes!"

An angel asked a girl to be Jesus's mother. Her name was Mary. She said yes

Vocabulary Words: yes.

Listening Words: asked, mother, angel

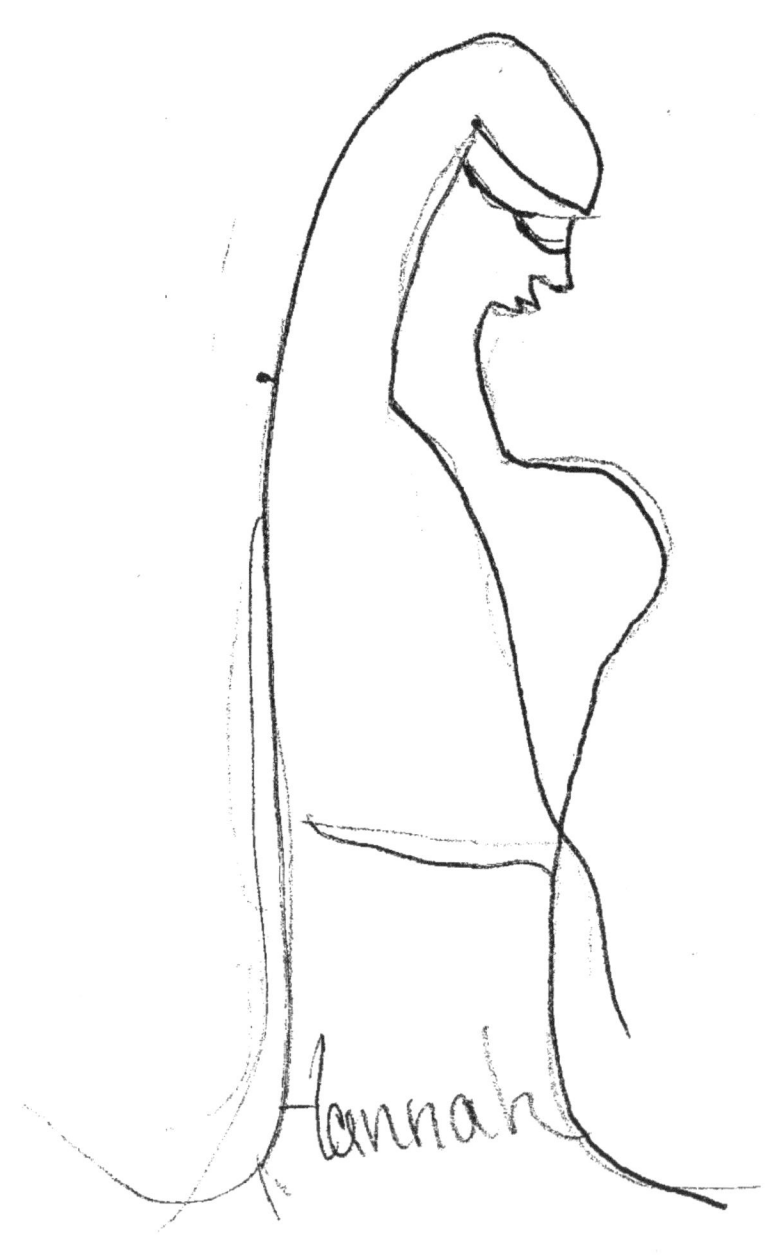

Women in the Bible

"Hannah"

She kept her faith in God and He answered her prayers.
She was once sad and then joyful.

Vocabulary Words: kept, she, sad, God

Listening Words: prayers, answered, faith

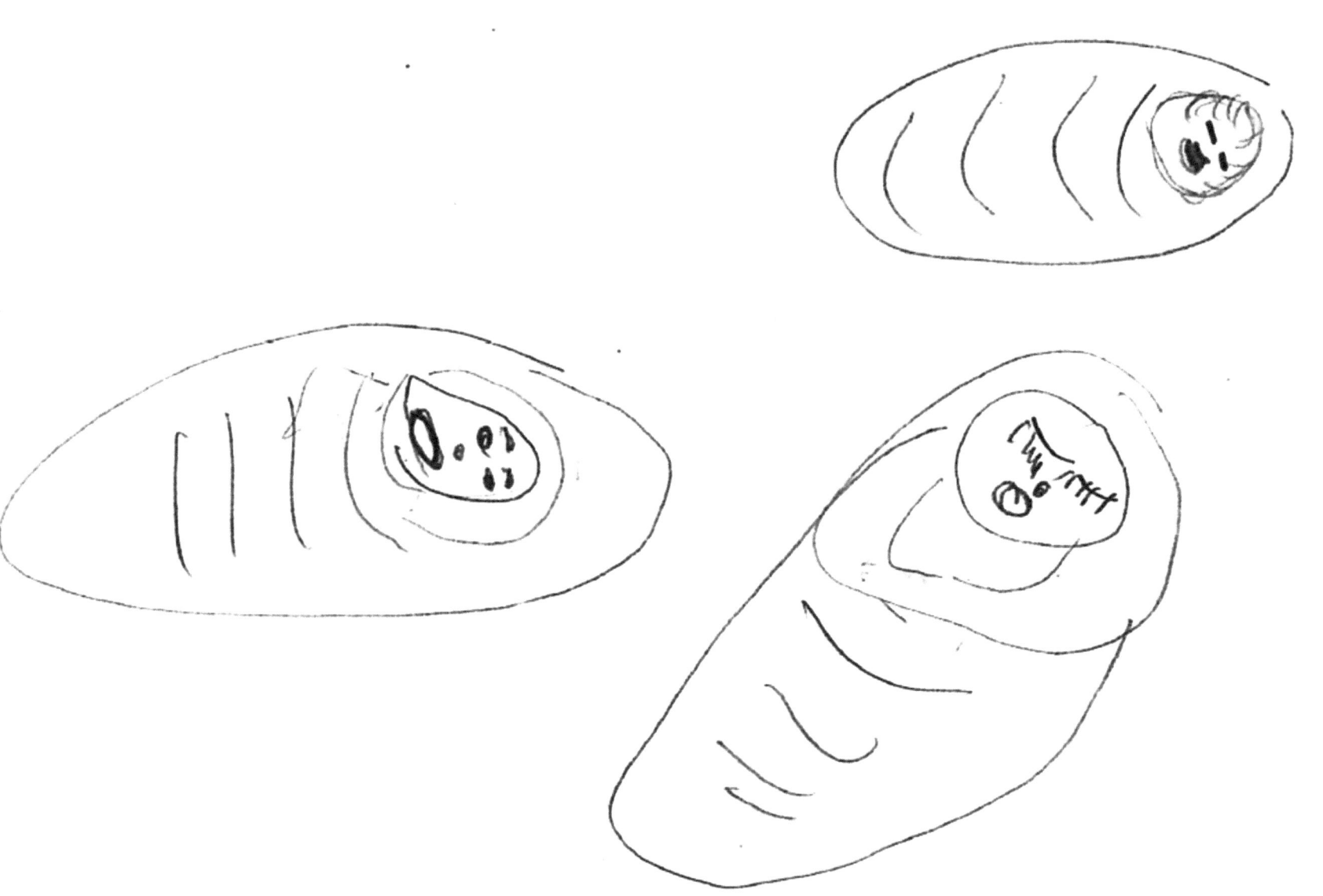

Women in the Bible

"Shiphrah and Puah"

Both women saved babies that were in danger.

Vocabulary Words: both, that, in

Listening Words: saved, babies, danger

Women in the Bible

"Mother Mary Visits Her Cousin Saint Elizabeth"

Mary and Elizabeth were cousins. They were expecting babies at the same time. Mary named her baby Jesus. Elizabeth named her baby John. Jesus and John helped people love God.

Vocabulary Words: love, help, visit, her

Listening Words: cousins, babies, named, expecting

ESTHER

Women in the Bible

"Queen Esther"

Esther loved her people by asking a king to spare their lives.

Vocabulary Words: king, land, her

Listening Words: spared, lives

Nature

"Garden of Eden"

The birds sang. The fish swam. The sun and moon and stars were bright. The land was green. The sky and sea were blue. They were happy. God was happy.

Vocabulary Words: fish, sea, sky, blue, love, God, land

Listening Words: happy, garden, birds, green

BLOW

Nature

"Calming the Wind"

The waves were large. The men were scared.
Jesus made the waves calm.

Vocabulary Words: men, waves, high, calm

Listening Words: scared

Relatives

"My Father's House"

Jesus was about 12 years old when he stayed at the temple extra days.
He was learning about God in the temple.
A temple teacher is called a rabbi.

Vocabulary Words: days

Listening Words: learning, temple, extra, rabbi

St Joachim
St Anne

the parents of the Blessed Virgin Mother Mary

Relatives

"St. Joachim and St. Anne"

They were the parents of Blessed Mother Mary and Grandfather and Grandmother to Jesus!

Vocabulary Words: Jesus

Listening Words: grandfather, grandmother

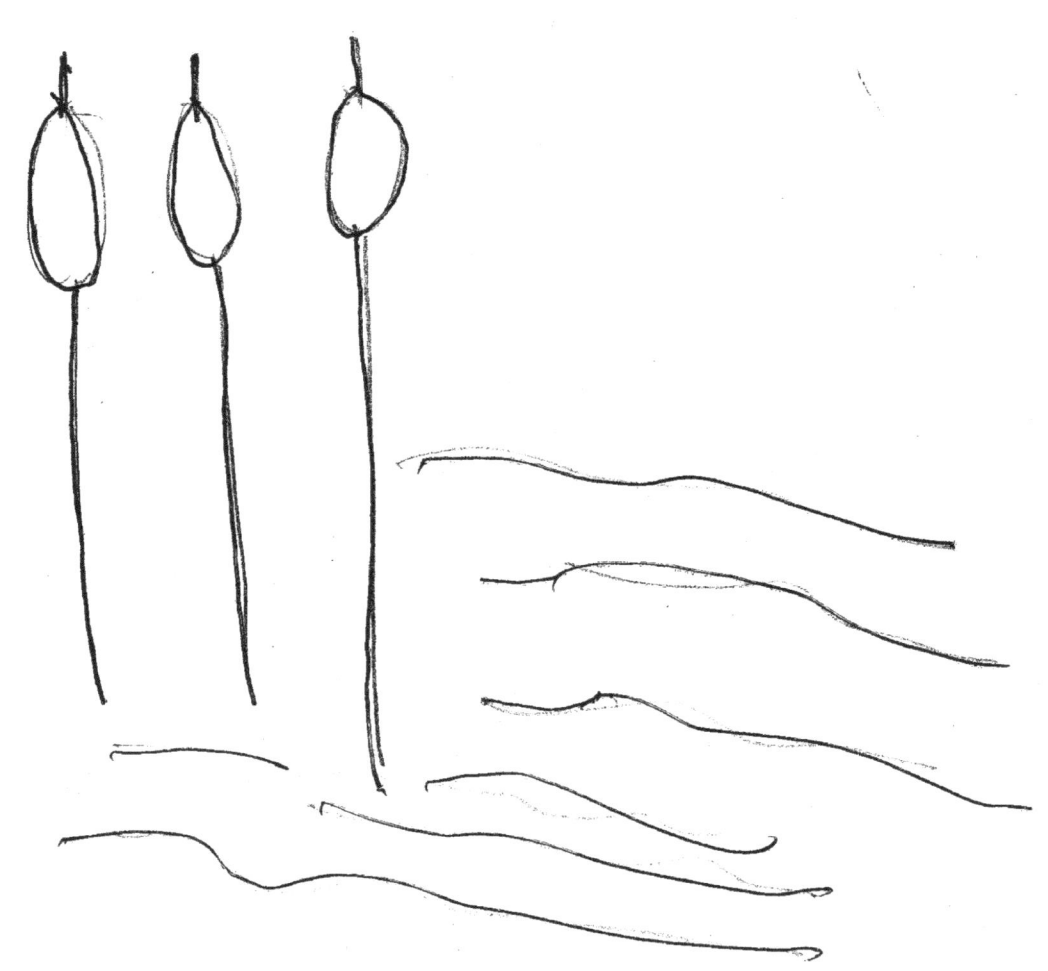

Closing Pages

"Moses and Reeds on the River"

About the Authors

Alice Boschulte Murray earned her undergraduate and graduate degrees from Fordham University in Education, Administration, and Supervision. She obtained several licenses including the New York City Board of Education Special Education license and has worked for over 25 years in various positions including supervisor, and administrator, within the New York City Board of Education. She earned a permanent license as a CCD (Confraternity of Christian Doctrine or Catechism) instructor for the Archdiocese of New York. She is a proud mother, grandmother, and great-grandmother.

This book is a collaboration with her eldest daughter Diane Murray Ward.

Diane obtained her undergraduate degree from CUNY Brooklyn College in Anthropology and Philosophy and minored in pre-Medicine, and her graduate degree from New York University in Rehabilitation Counseling and has taught grades kindergarten through adult learners.

This book is based on her work as a permanent licensed CCD instructor with early elementary-aged children. She has worked in both the private and public sectors. She is a written and spoken word poet appearing within national and international venues. She is a daughter, sibling, wife, mother, and friend.

Acknowledgments

Thank you to Bianca (Nandi) Jacob Stephenson for the assistance with the formatting and encouragement in producing "God's Love."

www.ingramcontent.com/pod-product-compliance
Lightning Source LLC
Chambersburg PA
CBHW041644070526

44585CB00004B/126